A MOTHER AND GRANDMOTHER'S LOVE

CAROLYN WILSON

Copyright ©2022 Carolyn Wilson

Published by: Dream Faith Publishing

www.dream-faith.com

TM

Library Congress Control Number: 2022912913

ISBN: 9798985303278

Printed in the United States

TABLE OF CONTENTS

Dedication 1

Chapter 1 " Decisions" 2

Chapter 2 "Misty's Pregnant" 15

Chapter 3 "The Hassle" 30

Chapter 4 "Guardianship" 41

Chapter 5 "A Mother's Love" 54

Chapter 6 "Marriage" 63

Chapter 7 "A Grandmother's Love" 87

Chapter 8 "The Best Lawyer 114

Money Could Buy"

DEDICATION

I would like to dedicate this book to all the mothers and grandmothers that have extended family members that causes chaos in your family. I encourage you to never ever give up on spending as much time as possible with your grandchildren. They need you to be a part of their lives. Don't take time for granted just because they are young. Sometimes, we must step up even when we don't feel like it or don't think we can do it!

Remember all your help comes from the Lord (Psalm 121:1). No matter what method God used to bring your grandchild/grandchildren into your life. Don't let someone else dictate what role you play in their lives. Regardless of how you're being treated by other adults participating. Refuse to exit your grandchild/grandchildren's lives. Let's be sure to take care of them. God is always watching.

Chapter 1

Decisions

During Misty's last year of high school, she moved out of state, because her parents were in the military. Her dad received orders to report to Hunter Airforce Base, located in Georgia. Misty had a strong supporting family that she could always depend on. She had an older sister, named Rolanda, who had joined the armed forces already, following in her dad's footsteps. Her Dad was due for retirement soon. Misty decided once she graduated, her career choice was joining the armed forces like her dad and big sister.

Once her parents got moved and settled into their new home, Misty was ready for her first day at the new high school. When she arrived, she didn't know anyone there, so she was very quiet. On the second day, she met a student by the name of Joanne! Joanne was a troubled child who saw Misty as a target; being a new kid in town! Misty didn't know anything about Joanne. She was more excited about making new friends.

Joanne approached Misty in one of their classes together. That's how she found out that Misty was a new student. Joanne was one of the first students to introduce herself to Misty, and after that she and Joanne became very good friends. Not in a good way!

One day Misty's mother, Sharon, got a call from the principal's office. "Principal Joe was letting Sharon know that Misty had gotten into some trouble with Joanne." Sharon asked, "if Misty was in the office and if she could speak with her?" "To which he agreed and passed the phone to Misty." "Sharon spoke briefly to Misty about the situation she had gotten herself into." "As soon as Sharon hung up the phone from talking to Misty, she called her husband and told him the principal wanted to see them both as soon as possible to talk about the concern he has involving Misty's behavior!"

Both of Misty's parents met up at the school to find out what had happened. Once they arrived and saw her in the principal's office, they were not happy at all. When the principal explained everything in full detail, they were surprised and shocked. Misty and Joanne were involved in an incident with a stolen electronic device. "Misty's parents informed Principal Joe that Misty had no reason to steal from anyone." "He told them that she wasn't the one who stole the device, it was Joanne!" "Misty was in trouble by association."

"Principal Joe said to her parents!" "I'm aware that Misty is a new student of ours that just transferred." "Sometimes when new students arrive in a new environment, they become targets!" "Others will try to befriend them with not so good intentions in mind, because they know that the new student doesn't know anything about them nor their character." "That happens a lot!"

"I have talked to Misty about choosing her friends wisely." "She seems to understand what I meant by the statement of friends!" He added. "I see that she has good grades and has never been in trouble from her previous school before now." "I'm sure that she will do well here and make better choices." "He went on to tell them how Misty explained that Joanne asked, "her to go into the P.E. room with her, but didn't know Joanne was going to steal anything."

After that incident, Misty stopped all contact with Joanne and focused more on her grades. Once Misty realized that the incident could have had really bad consequences, she made up her mind to make better choices and move forward. Misty was determined to graduate and finish high school in the first semester. She was able to enjoy a lot during her senior year of high school; from picking out her dress for prom, to hanging out with her new-found friends. She was happy and enjoying her life.

Misty got a job working at McDonalds. She was trying to show her dad that she could be responsible by holding down a job while keeping up her grades in school. Misty had really turned herself around! She would attend school from seven-forty-five in the morning, until two-thirty in the afternoon, then worked from four to eight. It allowed her to get enough sleep and prepare for school the next morning. Once the semester was over, Misty had all the credits needed to meet graduation requirements during her first semester just like she wanted. That meant, she didn't have to return to school after the holidays. Misty only had to return for graduation practice and set up a time with the photographer for senior portraits.

When it came to prom night, Misty was given a curfew to be home by eleven o'clock. She arrived home at nine! She told her parents "She didn't need to stay out that late." "All she wanted to do was eat supper with her date and go back home." Misty was excited that she had a chance to go to prom considering her older sister didn't have the privilege of going during her senior year of high school. On the other hand, while she was free to do whatever she wanted until graduation, she decided to change her hours at the job from the afternoon to mornings; replacing the hours she would have had at school. Not only was she working, but she also decided to join the armed forces training camp for future soldiers. Yes! Misty had gotten busy and was trying to make better decisions. This is the career path Misty wanted to take after graduating high school.

Soon she went on to graduate; after that she continued participating in the future soldier training program preparing her for the armed forces. She was still working at McDonalds. Misty wanted to be independent after she graduated, so she moved out of her parents' house on her own until it was time for her to report to basic training only after she completed the program. She and Rolanda even decided to share an apartment together. Misty seems to be making some impressive and mature decisions.

After a short time on her own, Misty met this young man by the name of Michael. Michael had never been introduced to Misty's family and she chose to keep it that way. Not to Soon after that! Misty started slacking up from her job and training with her recruiter. She was feeling tired and sleepy all the time; to the point where it was very noticeable. "When Misty's mom found out she told Misty that she was moving to the new duty station with them." Yes, they had to move again. Rolanda would be going with them as well. Her contract with the armed forces had ended and she would not be re-enlisting.

When they arrived at the new duty station, they settled in, and Rolanda got a job. Misty was trying to get a job, but no luck. She ended up staying home with her mom. "When Rolanda got off from work Misty asked if she could talk to her?" Rolanda said, "yes!" "Misty told her that she was feeling sick." Rolanda asked her "if she was pregnant?" "Misty didn't know, so she asked Rolanda if she would pick up a pregnancy test for her?" "To which Rolanda agreed to do so." After work the next day!

Rolanda kept her word and brought Misty the pregnancy test. Misty read and followed the directions on how to use it. Once she figured out one line meant negative, and two lines meant positive. They waited for about five minutes, then they checked the stick together and saw that it had two lines. She was pregnant!

Misty was so upset. She didn't know how to tell her parents; especially since she was only sixteen years old. Michael was twenty-one! Misty had graduated early but she was still a minor! When Sharon found out, she was not happy at all. She was sad and very disappointed in Misty.

Sharon wanted Misty to stay on her career path, but she didn't know how Misty would be able to do that now! Misty was turning into a young woman in a blink of an eye. She had just graduated high school and a month later she's pregnant! Sharon was trying to digest all of this before Misty's Dad found out. "Misty knew that her dad would be really upset, so she asked her mom to tell her dad that she was pregnant." "Her mom said no!" "you're going to put your big girl panties on and tell your dad yourself!" "Misty went into the room and told her dad that she was pregnant." He just looked at Misty and didn't say a word. She turned around and walked out the room.

When Misty got back outside where Rolanda and her mom was, they asked, "what did he say?" She stated with tears in her eyes, "he just looked at me and said nothing." "Her mom told her that she has to give her dad time to process it all, and that she was still considered *"dad's little girl."* He's just really hurt, give him time, her mom said." After which during several months of Misty's pregnancy, "she mentioned to her mom that Michael hadn't told his parents yet." She thought maybe he was trying to keep the pregnancy a secret from his parents.

Misty had so many mixed emotions, because Michael kept putting it off or would have some excuse on why he hadn't told them yet. She just didn't understand why it was taking Michael so long to inform his parents about the pregnancy. Sharon was also upset with Michael and had grown very impatient. She even thought to just take matters into her own hands. Then months went by, and Misty was seven months pregnant. Meanwhile trying to give Michael a chance to tell his parents. She felt that it was important that their child knew both sides of their family, with that being said Misty made the decision to fly back and have the baby in the same city as the dad, so that he could be a part of the child's life and the child would have the opportunity to have both parents. When she arrived, she found an apartment and informed Michael that she was in town. "She then asked him again had he told his parents about the pregnancy?" He stated, "not yet!"

By the eighth month of Misty's pregnancy, she decided that she would go to Michael's house to have a talk with his mom. She wanted to see if Michael had mentioned to them anything about expecting a baby with her. Misty wanted his parents to know about the pregnancy before she gave birth, not after!! When she made it to Michael's parents' house, she knocked on the door. His mom answered, and Misty introduced herself. Michael's mom seemed to have her guard up from the moment she opened the door. Misty introduced herself and told his mom who she was.

As Misty stood at the door, she started talking to her about the pregnancy... Michael's mother told her that "Michael had never mentioned anything to her about Misty at all, and to her knowledge he had not mentioned anything to his dad either." Michael's mom said, "that she appreciated Misty coming by to inform her about the pregnancy, and that she would speak to Michael when he returned home." However, later that evening as Misty and Michael were having a conversation on the phone, "he mentioned that he actually had told his dad previously, he just didn't tell his mother, because he felt that she was very sensitive about certain situations." "Michael told Misty to make sure she let him know when she was getting ready to have the baby, because he and his dad wanted to be at the hospital when she went into labor." Misty's big sister wanted to be with her in the delivery room too, although she was ten hours away, and had already decided that she wasn't going to miss it for the world.

Rolanda packed her car the morning Misty had gone into labor and got on the road. This was her first nephew, and she was going to be a Tete! Rolanda was so happy for her sister that she went and purchased everything that a baby could ever need for the first five months of its life. The little bundle of joy was coming into this world with so much love surrounding him. Rolanda got on the road and made it in the delivery room just in time to see Misty give birth to her first child. She took pictures and sent them to their mom. Rolanda and

13

Misty shared a bond like no other. Though they were five years apart, Rolanda had always felt that she had to be her sister's keeper. Rolanda always had Misty's back no matter what. Once the baby was born, Michael and his dad went into the room. They took one look at the beautiful baby boy, and both knew he was Michael's son.

"Michael's dad said that the baby looked just like Michael when he was a baby." Michael suggested that Misty name the baby after him to keep the legacy of the family name alive through generations to come. After all, Michael's parents only had one son. Misty hadn't named the baby yet, but she was thinking about the perfect name. However, she had already decided that she was not naming him after his father, even though he and his dad wanted her too. She finally chose the name that felt right to her. She named him Jordan.

Chapter Two

Misty's Pregnant

Jordan was such a sweetie pie. Before Michael's dad left the hospital, he told Misty that if she ever needed anything for the baby at all just let him know and he will make sure that she gets it. He also told her that he was going to drop off a few things by her apartment to have when she makes it home from the hospital. Misty kindly thanked him.

Michael was so excited! This was his first child. He stayed at the hospital with Misty and gave Jordan his first bath. He didn't leave Misty's side. When it came time for Misty and Jordan to go home, Michael went with them. Michael ended up moving into the apartment that Misty and Rolanda shared. Michael's dad kept his word and did exactly what he said he would do, with the help of Rolanda. They both had a surprise waiting for Misty. The moment she stepped into her room she saw balloons, her favorite movie "The Breaking of Dawn", and a few items for Jordan on her bed.

After a few weeks had passed, Misty's parents decided it was time they stop by to meet the young man that their daughter had fallen head over heels for. Although John had never met Michael, he felt that his actions had spoken loud enough so, he really didn't care to meet him. John's exact words were "Misty was too young to be having a baby at this point and time in her life." John blamed Michael because he was more experienced than his baby girl.

Misty was just sixteen at the time she became pregnant. He felt she was on her way to securing a career for herself. John felt that Michael was trying to take advantage of his baby girl. But John had to put all of that aside to congratulate Misty who wasn't such a baby girl anymore but had become a young woman early in her life with her own baby boy.

Once Sharon and John got to Rolanda and Misty's apartment to see little Jordan, they didn't have much of an idea of what they would say to Michael. They decided too just be themselves. Once they got inside, the trio was sitting on the couch: Misty, Michael, and baby Jordan. Regardless of how Misty's parents felt about the situation, they were mature enough to set aside all those feelings for the sake of their daughter and new grandson. They chose to have nothing but positive energy around the baby.

As they engaged in conversation with Michael, they asked him general questions about himself and his parents. Michael even offered up his mom's phone number for Sharon to call her and get an introduction over the phone. Misty's parents had just moved back from Texas to Georgia. While Michael's mom was residing in their new home in Florida, his dad resided in Georgia as well. He couldn't move until he found another job in Florida or closer to Florida. Michael's dad commuted every other weekend to see his wife, who would continue living there alone.

One night as Sharon was sitting home alone, she decided to give Michael's mom a call. She felt that she could relate to her situation, as for as living in a big empty house all by herself and being so far away from family. She knew that living alone wasn't easy.

As Sharon dialed the number, she contemplated on what she would say to someone that she had never met, but she understood that they had one thing in common and that was Jordan. When Michael's mom answered the phone, Sharon said, "Hello, my name is Sharon!" "I'm Misty's mom." "I hope that you don't mind me calling?" "How are you doing?" "Michael had given me your phone number, so I could call and check on you." "He thought by reaching out to you we may be able to form some type of friendship." "I know that you don't know me like that, but maybe someday we can get together."

Michael's mom replied saying, "I'm Brenda, and it's so good that you reached out to me." "I kind of stay to myself a lot." "I haven't lived here long." "My husband and I moved here about a month ago." "He travels back and forth every other weekend."

Sharon then asked Brenda, "if she was okay staying there by herself?" "She told Sharon how excited she is when Misty and Michael bring Jordan to visit her and stay overnight, especially when her husband isn't there." "Sharon then extended the invitation for Brenda to call her if she needed someone to talk to every now and again." "Brenda told her that she would, and the conversation ended."

The next day Misty called her mom and told her that Michael's mom had called her and asked if she and Michael could come live with her. Brenda told Misty, "That she would help them with Jordan while they looked for work, so they wouldn't have to pay anyone to watch him if they found a job." The only thing she asked, "is that they contribute while living with her." "Brenda told Misty and Michael that she has plenty of room for them to stay."

"Brenda told Misty that she has four bedrooms and three that no one is sleeping in. She also shared with Misty that she could have her own room." All Sharon could say to Misty was, "Well, you're grown now, so if you feel like you want to do that and can find a job there to stay independent for yourself, then I'm behind you every step of the way." "But aren't you training for a new position where you already work?"

Misty said, "yes but she was going to try and transfer once they moved in with Michael's mom." Sharon didn't tell her, but she didn't like the idea of Misty moving in with Michael's mom one bit. She felt as though it would cripple Misty. She didn't want that to cause Misty to lose out on her independence. She also felt like it wasn't ok for Brenda to ask Misty to give up everything and move into her house with her son when they weren't married. Sharon just couldn't understand that for anything. *"Who does that?"* she thought. *"Just tell me what kind of parent lets a baby momma move in with the baby daddy, and they're not married?"*

After all was said and done, Misty made her decision to move. She quit her job and followed Michael to his parents' house in Florida. Which was about six hours away from her family. Misty felt that she would get to know a little bit more about Michael and his family by moving in with them. She wanted her family to work. She looked at her parents as great role models and hoped to build a similar life with Michael. She was going to do whatever it took to try and make her relationship work and she believed that someday Michael would ask for her hand in marriage.

Misty's mom was an old school type of person. She felt that some things were just crossing the line. Sharon knew she had to let Misty make her own choices in life, but it wasn't easy. Misty had a family now and if staying with Michael and his parents to form a relationship with them is what she wanted, then Sharon had to accept that decision and move on.

Once Misty got to Michael's parents' house and settled in, the first thing she started focusing on was a job: that was her mission! Misty didn't want to live with anyone and not be able to contribute financially. She wanted to show Brenda and her husband that she wasn't a person that just sits around the house using her child as an excuse for not having a job. She wanted them to know that she was the kind of person that was always trying to better herself in this society. Misty was putting in application after application but couldn't land anything. She even tried getting a transfer from where she worked in Georgia. Michael was trying to find a job also, but there was no success for him either. Misty was feeling down and disappointed in herself because she just wasn't the kind of person to sit around and do nothing.

Misty decided to call her mom and express to her how she was feeling about the situation she had found herself in with not being able to find a job. She said that Michael's parents didn't have enough food to support all of them, and that she needed to get food for her and Jordan. Misty felt embarrassed to ask her mother for money. But of course; Sharon sent money to help take care of her and Jordan. Sharon loved her daughter and grandson so she had no problem helping, but eventually she became a little overwhelmed and worried because she had no idea that she would have to constantly send money to Misty for food week after week. Misty had always been independent since high school and has never had to ask her parents for money.

Misty got tired of asking her mom to send money for food because she couldn't seem to find a job. "Misty told her mom that she was applying for jobs outside of fast-food chains but, they were just not hiring." After a few months of Misty living in the house with Michael and his parents, she figured she needed to go back home. "When Misty woke up one morning and decided that she would tell Michael that she was going to move back home." "She felt that she could no longer continue to live like she'd been living, and it was too much for her to handle not having a job to support Jordan or herself."

A few days later, Misty felt sick and went to the doctor. When she made it to the doctor's office, she could barely walk, because of the stomach pain. The doctor took blood samples and other tests to find out what was going on with Misty. When the test results came in, "Misty was told that she was pregnant." Misty was shocked to hear those words come out of the doctor's mouth and asked was he sure? He told Misty yes that, he was sure. After that Misty didn't have anything else to say. She left the doctor's office with her head down feeling so disappointed in herself *like how did she let this happen!*

Misty went back to Michael's parents' house and told him that she was pregnant with their second child. "She told him that he would need to tell his parents that she is pregnant." They knew she had gone to the doctor to find out why she was feeling ill, so she was sure that they'd ask what the Dr. say?" Michael's dad was away at work, but his mom was home sitting in the family room watching T.V. "Michael asked his mother if he could speak with her in private?" "To which she invited him to sit." He sat down beside his mom and told her that Misty was pregnant. Brenda had a look of shock on her face! she called Misty in to ask her if it was true? Misty confirmed by saying, yes!"

"Brenda then told Michael to step out of the room while she and Misty had a conversation." Michael left so they could talk. "Brenda then proceeded to ask Misty how she got pregnant and who was the father?" Of course, "Misty said the baby was Michael's." "Brenda went on to tell her that she would only be able to help with Jordan and that she wasn't going to be able to help her with both kids."

Misty was furious at the nerve of this woman! In her mind. But she went on to reply, "That's fine." "I'll be able to take care of my own kids because I'm moving back home with my sister in the apartment we shared." "I'll also be able to get my old job back." "I've already called and was able to speak with the manager there." "You all can call to check on Jordan whenever you feel like it."

"I understand that you're moving back, but Michael isn't going to follow you back this time!" Brenda rebutted. "He will be staying here with me!" Misty's reply to Brenda was one word.

"Okay."

When their conversation was over, Misty went to talk to Michael. "She asked Michael if he and his mom had already been discussing what would happen if she ever decided to leave and go back home?"

Michael replied, "yes!"

"So, did you and your mother decided or did your mother decide that you weren't going back to be with me and your only son?"

"Yea…," Michael replied. "It was me and my mother's decision!"

Irritated, hurt, and angry, Misty continued. "Michael, you're a grown man, and you're just going to listen to what your mom says without even talking to me about it?" "We came here together." "We shouldn't have ever moved in with your parents." We were doing just fine with the three of us before I let your mom talk us into coming here with her." "So, I guess our relationship is over!" Michael didn't say anything.

Misty was heartbroken, disappointed, and didn't know what else to say. Although she did have one more question that needed to be asked before she went to pack up her belongings. "She wanted to know why Michael was choosing to stay with his mom in a place where he couldn't even get a job, instead of coming back with his family?" "Michael told Misty that he and his parents have had an estranged relationship for a while and that he had been messing up a lot." He felt that now they have allowed him back into the house he needed to stay in their good graces because his mom told him that if he leaves again, to never come back!"

He went on to tell Misty; "She said that I wouldn't be able to come back for anything so, I felt that; out of all the trouble I've been in and caused them, I didn't want to be another disappointment to her."

"But you can't be a man and step up to fatherhood?" Misty argued. "For your son and our other child, we have on the way?"

Michael stated, "I love my mom, and she's here living in this house by herself because my dad has not found a job close enough to move back yet… and you don't have to leave and move back with the kids alone." He retaliated. "That's something you want to do on your own."

"Michael, neither one of us can get a job anywhere here." "What am I supposed to do for money?" Says Misty. I can't "keep asking my mom for money."

"I refuse to keep living day to day like this; wondering where the next meal is going to come from!" "I was not raised that way!" "I have to get out and be able to provide for my kids." "The people around here are just not giving us a job." "It's not that they're not hiring, they're just not hiring us, and I don't know why." Misty turns around and walks away.

Chapter Three

The Hassle

Now that the decision had officially been made that Misty was leaving. She began packing her and Jordan's belongings. After packing Michael helped by putting her and Jordan's suitcases into her car. Brenda didn't have any emotional expressions at all as Misty was getting ready to leave. Jordan was Brenda's first-born grandson, so Misty didn't understand why it seemed like Brenda was just too glad to see them leave. Misty drove off leaving Michael with the reassurance that she will still call him, and that they'll have to see how their relationship plays out with them living in two different states and all.

When Misty made it back to the apartment she and Rolanda shared, "she called Michael to let him know that she and Jordan had made it home safely." "She told Michael that she would bring Jordan to visit him on some of her weekends off or he can always come and spend as much time with Jordan as he would like." Once she unloaded everything out of the car, she went to speak with the manager at Office Depot to let him know that she had made it back in town and to find out what day and time he wanted her to report to work.

Don, the manager, "told Misty that she could start the upcoming Monday, since it was Friday to give her a couple days to rest." "Misty agreed and thanked him." He let Misty know how much she was missed, and they were excited to have her back. "He stated to her that she is such a hard-working employee, and as long as he is the manager over the store, she would always have a job." He only expected her to keep up the great work with her customer service and professionalism.

Once Misty had gotten back into the routine, it was just like she had never left. The first weekend Misty was off, "Michael called and asked her if it was okay to come pick up Jordan and take him back for a while." "Misty responded that it was fine with her."

Jordan was only three months old at the time. She thought it was a great thing that his father wanted to help with him by taking him for a little while. She was able to go back to work full force after that weekend off. From that day on Misty worked every day, never missing a shift unless she or Jordan had a doctor's appointment. Misty was a very dependable and hard-working employee. She did what she had to do to support her son. She would also work extra hours to help her co-workers and would go in if anyone called out.

About two weeks had passed since Michael picked up Jordan. Misty had begun to miss him badly. So, "she decided to call and ask Michael when he would be bringing Jordan back home?" "He told her that he wasn't bringing him back and that she would have to come pick him up if she wanted him." Misty was upset! "She explained to

Michael that wasn't the conversation they had agreed upon before he and his mother left with Jordan." Michael didn't care to hear anything that Misty had to say. He had spoken his peace in reference to the matter.

Misty was not happy. "She told Michael that she would be there to pick Jordan up on her next day off." When the time had come for Misty to go and bring Jordan back, she was met with nothing but hassle. When she made it to Michael's, she knocked on the front door. Michael asked, "who it was?" There was no answer, but he slowly went to the door. "As he opened the door and saw that it was Misty, he asked "what she wanted?" As if he didn't already know that she was coming.

Misty asked, "to see her son?" "Michael told her no!" Misty couldn't understand why Michael was treating her as if he didn't have a clue as to why she was there and what was going on! Sharon certainly didn't like the fact that Misty had let Jordan leave with them traveling so many hours away in the first place, but there was nothing for her to say to Misty that would change her mind. Although she felt like Jordan was too young to be staying so far away from his mom with him being only 3 months old.

"Michael told Misty she couldn't see Jordan and changed his mind about letting Jordan leave." Michael was trying to keep Misty away from her son, he wasn't going to allow her to take Jordan back home. Instead, "he told Misty that he wanted Jordan to stay a few more weeks and then he would bring him to her." Misty felt that it was absurd for Michael to try and not let her see her son after she had driven so far to pick him up. He could have called her and had that conversation over the phone.

"Misty then called her mom and told her that she had driven all those miles for nothing, and that Michael and his mom would be bringing Jordan back in about three weeks." However, by the time week two arrived, "Misty got a phone call from Michael saying that he was not going to be able to bring Jordan back." "He arrogantly told Misty that if she wanted Jordan back, then she would have to come pick him up herself!" Misty was not pleased. She said, ``This would be the second time you have told me this." As the conversation continued between them, the tension kept accumulating. The conversation ended with Misty, "telling Michael that she was going to pick up her son on her next weekend off and that she will do whatever she has to do to bring her son home." This'll be another long drive in the attempt and hopes of getting her son.

When the weekend had finally come, Misty headed out in the early part of the morning to try and get her son for the second time once again. When she had made it to her destination; she stepped out of the car, headed to the door, and rang the doorbell. This time Michael's mom answered the door. When she saw that it was Misty, she cracked it only a little bit between the two of them.

Misty could barely see anything as she was peeping inside the door to see if she was going to get a glimpse of Jordan. She couldn't see anything at all. Brenda yelled for Michael to let him know that Misty was at the front door for him, without asking Misty to come inside. She left her standing out in the cold while she waited to speak with Michael and pick up her son.

When Michael made it outside, he didn't have Jordan with him. Misty asked, "where Jordan was?" "So that she could hurry up and get back on the road." "Michael said to Misty for the second time that he didn't know why she drove all the way there to pick up Jordan because she was not getting him." Michael had Misty under the impression that she was picking up her son this time. Misty has begun to realize that they were trying to take her son away from her.

Misty was furious as she asked, "Michael why wasn't he giving her son back to her?" Michael wasn't giving Misty any answers as to why she couldn't get Jordan. Once again, he's repeating the same thing all over from their phone conversation, where he told her that if she wanted him back, she had to come and pick him up. They both stood outside in the cold arguing over Jordan until Misty got to the point where she asked, "Michael if she could at least see him?" Michael went inside the house to get Jordan.

All that back and forth with him just drained her. Misty had become exhausted and frustrated. At this point she just wanted to see her son. Misty decided that she would come up with a plan later to see what she needed to do to get Jordan back. She wanted to have this taken care of before the new baby was born.

Misty was so upset that she had driven all that way and had spent all that time on the road driving in hopes of picking up her son. Yet she wasn't even allowed to go inside their house to spend time with him. "How could they leave her out in the cold after she had lived with them?" Most would wonder what's really going on.

Misty knew something wasn't right with her sons' father. He would barely let her spend time with her son while she was there visiting. Michael wouldn't let Misty and Jordan out of his sight the whole time she was visiting as if she was a stranger to Jordan. The fact that he had her drive all the way there like that, not just one time but twice, knowing the whole time that he wasn't going to give up Jordan was a mischievous act. Misty was thankful on the other hand that she did get to spend a little time with Jordan. It was much too cold for Jordan and her to be outside, so they sat in her car. Michael had to be in there as well. He didn't have too, he chose too! He wasn't letting Misty make a step with Jordan without him being right there with them for every move they made. When Misty finished her visit with Jordan, it was time to head back home without her son once again. She was heartbroken! Leaving him behind.

As Misty went to work the next day, she talked to Don about what had occurred the weekend she went to pick up her son. Don hated to hear of all the turmoil Misty was going through. "She asked Don if she could request to be off the weekend coming up so that she could try and convince Michael to let her get Jordan." Don agreed to her having that weekend off and told her, if there's anything else he could do for her all she has to do is ask.

When Misty got off from work, "she called Michael on the phone and told him that she would be coming to pick Jordan up this weekend." "She told him that her family was giving her a baby shower and she wanted Jordan to be there!" Misty thought that she would give it one more try to get her son back from his father in a peaceful manner. Now for the third time, she hit the road again to get her son.

When she made it to Michael's parents' house, she knocked on the door and Michael answered with Jordan in his arms along with his clothes. Misty didn't waste any time getting her son and getting back on the road. She made it back safely and prepared for her baby shower. When the day of the baby shower finally came around, Misty's mom had prepared all the food and her sister coordinated the decorations and had gifts for the guests. Misty was so happy! Everything about that day turned out to be just what she needed; a lot of laughing, surrounded by family and friends. After it was all over Misty thanked everyone for coming. Her mom had gone and printed off pictures she had taken from the baby shower and made Misty a photo album as another gift for her to remember and cherish the joy of that day.

After a long and busy weekend, it was time for Misty to go back to work. Misty was trying to work as many hours as she could before the birth of her second baby. She wanted to be sure she had enough money saved up to survive off until she was released from under the doctors' care after birth. Even though she knew she could count on her family for all the support she would need, Misty didn't feel like it was their responsibility.

Chapter 4

Guardianship

Although Misty was working hard as a single parent to support herself and Jordan, she seemed to have forgotten about the one she was carrying; she worked a lot! Misty started having a difficult time carrying her second child. She had a lot of false labor pains that caused her to leave work early two to three times a week. When she started taking on extra shifts, it put her at risk. She had to be put on bed rest until the baby was born.

Rolanda was a big help for Misty; she made sure that Misty had everything that she needed for the delivery of her nephew as she did for Jordan.

When the time had come for Misty to have the baby, she was home alone sitting on the sofa when the contractions started. Rolanda had gone to take care of some personal business. The only other person Misty could think to call was her mom. Misty was telling her mom how close the contractions were getting. She also told her mom that the contractions had gotten stronger, and they were now 30 minutes apart. Her mom asked, "Misty if she'd been having contractions thirty minutes apart for an hour straight yet?" Misty replied, "no ma'am!" "She told Misty if she hadn't then she needed to sit for an extra hour in order to time the contractions." "If they were coming fifteen minutes apart or sooner then she needed to go to the hospital, because that meant she was in labor."

Misty had gone full term with her first pregnancy. Now it was time for this little bundle of joy to arrive, but no one was there to drive Misty to the hospital. With her sister gone and her mom not being there either.

Misty had one or two choices. She could either call 911 for an ambulance, or she could attempt to drive herself to the hospital. She chose option number two. Yes! Misty chose to drive herself. God allowed Misty to drive herself safely to the Women and Children's Hospital. Misty called Rolanda while enroute to the hospital to let her know that she was in labor and to meet her at the hospital.

When Rolanda met Misty at the hospital. Misty asked, "Rolanda to take out her phone and video the entire birth." Rolanda did exactly what Misty asked of her, she pulled out her phone and began to record! Misty had already decided on a name for the baby. She knew earlier along in her pregnancy what the gender of her baby was going to be during her well baby checkups. His name is going to be Darius! When Darius came into this world, he was surrounded by a lot of love and positive energy. Michael wasn't present for the birth of his now second baby boy with Misty. He and Misty now share two sons together. Misty was a bit disappointed that Michael couldn't make it for the second baby's birth. However, Rolanda was there; she wouldn't have missed it for anything in the world. She had stopped everything just to meet Misty at the hospital. When Misty asked her, "where she had been and what she was doing?" Rolanda explained, "that she was doing some last-minute shopping for the baby." Honestly, it didn't really matter to Misty what Rolanda was in the middle of doing. She was just grateful that her sister made it for the birth of her nephew.

Misty had to stay a couple days in the hospital after giving birth to Darius. While she was in the hospital recuperating from giving birth, "Brenda called Misty on the phone asking her to sign guardianship papers concerning Jordan, so that she and her husband could put Jordan on their health insurance." Jordan had health insurance which wouldn't allow coverage for him if he became sick while visiting them. "She went on to explain telling

Misty that Jordan would also be covered with their insurance when they travel to visit other family members as well." "Brenda continued to emphasize that if Jordan got sick; it wouldn't be a problem for him to go anywhere to see a doctor and be treated." "She explained it would only be for a year and a couple of months."

"Misty told Brenda that she would have to think about it." This subject was not something she wanted to hear or talk about over the phone with Michael's mom, especially after just giving birth. She was still in the hospital, and to hear such a proposal was just too overwhelming; especially with all the turmoil she had just gone through with them already.

Rolanda made sure that Misty didn't want for anything, just as she had done for Jordan. Rolanda brought receiving blankets to the hospital, including clothes that baby Darius would need before going home. After dropping the items off to Misty, Rolanda left the hospital for a little while to get Misty's room ready for their return home. She wanted everything to be perfect for Misty and baby Darius.

Rolanda had bought everything from the bottle warmer to a diaper genie. When Misty made it home from the hospital, she told Rolanda that she really appreciated everything she had done for her.

Rolanda replied, "You're welcome!" "You're my little sister and I will always have your back no matter what!" "I will be here for you anytime you need me, even though you can be a bit selfish at times." "I'm not just going to leave you hanging knowing that you need help."

Misty simply thanked her, but her heart was flooded with emotions of love and appreciation.

Rolanda and Misty lived across town from their parents. "Sharon told Misty that when she wanted to return to work, she could enroll the boys in childcare at the facility where she worked." The facility didn't accept children less than 6 weeks old,

Darius was only day's old, so she had to wait a little longer to enroll him.

Before you knew it Jordan had turned a year old, and Darius was 2 months old. While Misty sat at home with her boys she applied for other jobs, seeking additional employment. The money she was making at her current job was barely enough to take care of herself and two kids. After being back at work for about two weeks, Misty received a phone call for an interview at a call center where she filled out an application. She got the job!

Now that she has been hired for this new job, Misty had to go ahead and put the boys in childcare. Although the center requires an updated shot record, Misty new Darius wasn't caught upon all his shots, and it was going to cause a problem. She was trying to get his shots caught up and put on a blue card. When Misty went to enroll the boys for childcare at the same center her mom worked. The Director told Misty that she had five days to have the blue card in or she wouldn't be able to keep Darius enrolled.

The reason for Misty enrolling her boys at that childcare center, is only because her mom works there and would have extra help. She knew it would be more convenient for her mom to take the boys home with her every evening instead of having to get off work early to pick them up.

Misty had talked to Michael about how much childcare was going to cost for both boys to attend. Michael had assured Misty that he would pay half of the boys' tuition, but when time came to pay on the account, he never had the money. After several attempts to try and get Michael to honor his commitment, she faced disappointment after disappointment. So, she finally got to the point that she just gave up on asking him for anything. She was convinced that she just wouldn't have any help at all with the childcare bill.

Misty decided to take a different approach. She talked to Michael and told him about the new job at the call center. She told him that she hadn't started getting paid yet, but the hourly pay rate was much more than what she was making. She would just need help with the boys until she got her first paycheck. Michael told Misty that he could get the boys for a few weeks to help her out, but he was not sending her any money.

Misty was really upset about having to let her babies go so far away as little as they were, just because she couldn't afford the childcare fees alone. But, after giving it some thought, she realized that it might not be such a bad idea after all. She thought to herself, if *they go with their dad for those two weeks, that will give me a chance to work and get a few paychecks. Then I will be able to pay for childcare by the time they get back*."

Misty packed the boys up for the long drive. Her mom was not fond of the idea! She wished that there was another way to work things out to keep the boys with them. She felt that Michael had just come up with another way for Misty to give him the boys and that he'd do the same thing as before when it was time for them to come back home; not give them back.

The way he didn't want to let Jordan go with Misty when she had driven all that way to his house and the hard time, he gave her left a bad taste in her mouth. Sharon just didn't trust him at all, and she begged Misty to look into other solutions. But Misty was insistent that the boys would be ok with their dad for those two weeks. That made Sharon really distressed, because she just felt as if she wasn't going to see them anymore.

Michael and his parents came to pick up the boys. Darius didn't really know his dad because he hadn't been around him like Jordan had. Once the boys had left, Misty called Michael to check up on them, but he didn't answer the phone. Misty tried several more times afterwards, hoping that he would answer, but he never did. She started to wonder if she had made a mistake in trusting their dad with taking the boys for two weeks. Thankfully she was reassured after Michael called her back a few hours later to let her know that the boys were ok.

After about a week there had been some complications with the way Michael was handling the situation with the boys. Misty called to confirm that he would be bringing the boys back that following weekend. He told her that she was going to have to come pick them up herself. Misty went to talk to her parents about having to pick up the boys.

Once Misty got Michael on the phone to let him know that she would be coming, the conversation went left, and she told him that she was coming that weekend to pick up the boys.

When Misty and her parents arrived to pick up the boys, they looked terrible. Darius looked tired, and his ears were packed with a lot of hard crusty wax. Jordan looked really tired and out of it, like he didn't know what was going on. Sharon was really concerned about the way the boys looked once they got into the truck. Sharon tried to have small talk with the boys, but they were just so quiet.

Eventually after riding for about three hours they started to come around a little bit. Misty said that she wasn't going to let two-month-old Darius go back to visit with his dad anymore until he got older. Sharon was just happy that they were back home, and she didn't want either of them to go back. Darius had also gotten a REALLY BAD diaper rash. His bottom looked like the skin had been burned off. It was raw on both sides of his butt cheeks and around his whole bottom area. Sharon turned from being glad that the boys were back, to being very angry with their dad and other grandparents.

She couldn't understand what in the world had happened to little Darius in such a short time with them. Sharon was just horrified! When they got back home, Misty put the boys back into childcare. Darius was crying a lot because his bottom was hurting so badly. He had medicated cream to put on the infected areas, but it didn't seem to be working. Sharon tried putting Vaseline on the baby's bottom and that soothed him for a little while.

Jordan was in his Grandma Sharon's classroom at the daycare. She loved the idea of being able to spend all that time with her grandson especially while teaching her class. She treated Jordan just like the rest of the kids and she was careful to not give him any special treatment. When Jordan got a hug from his grandmother, the whole class got a hug too. It became her natural way of interacting with her class. They came to call it "giving the children a little TLC".

Chapter Five

A Mother's Love

Jordan and Darius stayed at the childcare center with Grandma Sharon, and for a while things were looking up for Misty. She was holding down a new job and taking care of her boys. She finally found a piece of the independence she had been missing. As time went on, she was still the only parent providing care for the boys. Their dad was still not able to help with childcare expenses. Although she wished he could pitch in a little bit, he didn't. Misty was handling everything on her own. Besides, she knew that he honestly didn't have anything to contribute. He was struggling to get a job. However, the childcare expenses became too much for Misty to pay alone for two kids. It was such a hardship to provide a roof over their heads, food to eat, and all the necessities needed for small children in addition to the childcare expenses. She knew that as a parent it was her responsibility to do all those things for her kids.

She was a very young parent, but she knew that her children depended on her for safety and security. Misty vowed to do everything she could do to protect and take care of her boys, no matter what it took or the sacrifices she had to make. In the past, before Misty had taken the new job, she was struggling with all the same issues. It seemed to her that these issues were becoming recurring instances. Misty shared her concerns with her mom, but Sharon was barely making enough to cover her own bills at that time. Regardless of Sharon's own personal struggles, she did her best to help Misty out with the childcare for the boys.

Misty had mentioned to her mom that she and the boys' father had been talking. He asked about getting Jordan for a while to help her out, because he couldn't help her with childcare and it was all he was able to do since he still didn't have a job. Sharon told Misty that she didn't want her to let Jordan stay so far away. She was afraid they would try to keep him again and she wouldn't be able to get him back. However, Misty didn't share the same concerns. She felt that it was going to be ok, and her mind was made up. She completely dismissed his arrogance!

Sharon was very disappointed because she didn't know when she would ever be able to see Jordan again. She felt that Michael and his parents wanted all or nothing and that they were going to trick Misty in some kind of way to keep Jordan, but Misty couldn't see that. She still thought they were nice people despite what had happened just a few months ago.

Misty also told her mom that Michael's parents had asked again about the guardianship papers concerning Jordan so he can have health care coverage.

"Misty, what do they need guardianship papers for?" Sharon questioned. "He is on Medicaid." "Why can't you just transfer his Medicaid?"

"I will let Mrs. Brenda know that I will be switching his Medicaid over before I let him go stay with them for a few weeks," Misty replied.

In about two weeks, Brenda and her husband came to pick up Jordan. Misty was working that day, so she asked her mom to meet Brenda and her husband at McDonald's. Sharon cared so much for Jordan and Darius. She didn't want to see them split apart, but at that time with Misty's situation she knew that her mind was made up and it didn't matter how anyone felt about the decision.

Misty had put in the paperwork for the transfer of the Medicaid card for Jordan. After about a week of applying for Jordan's Medicaid card, it was approved and had been sent out to Michael's address. When Misty asked Brenda if she received the Medicaid card for Jordan, she told Misty no, and that she had been looking for it in the mail. Misty wondered what was going on with it. Before you knew it, Jordan had been with his dad and Brenda for about three weeks, and still no card.

Soon Brenda decided to call Misty and ask her again about adding Jordan on to their private health insurance. They mentioned again to Misty that the only thing she needed to do was sign temporary guardianship papers so he could be added to their insurance. This way, Jordan could have surgery to fix his ears that folded over from not fully developed when he was born and would continue getting his asthma medication. They would also be able to get the hernia below his belly button taken care of. She said again that he had to be on it for at least a year and after a year he would be off.

Brenda told Misty that she and Michael would have to sign an agreement for the guardianship papers to be approved. The only reason Misty signed those papers was because she needed to have him covered with health insurance and wanted to make sure that Jordan would be taken care of. Misty was doing her best to try and do the right things for her boys. She was taking care of them the best way she could at the time. Misty was not going to give up on making sure her boys would be ok. When Misty told her mom that she had signed the guardianship papers, she was furious. As she had previously told Misty, she thought it was a bad idea, but she realized that Misty was going to do whatever she wanted to do and that she couldn't tell her anything as a grown woman. Sharon knew that she had raised her young lady well and that she had to accept the decisions Misty made were hers to make, she had to trust that God would be in control of everything.

After Misty signed those papers, Brenda reassured Misty that Jordan would be under their care for only one year and then the guardianship papers would no longer be valid. Misty believed every word that Brenda had told her. Soon Misty switched jobs and went into the field of childcare, though Misty worked at a different childcare facility from her mom. Misty was able to have Darius with her at the center she worked at. Darius had to be signed into the program just like every child enrolled, and there were no exceptions just because Misty worked there. However, Misty only had to pay fifty dollars a week.

She enjoyed working with the children, but she found herself once again neither being able to make enough money to live a comfortable lifestyle, nor receive affordable health insurance benefits for her boys. Misty thought long and hard about trying to pursue the military again as a career. She decided to go and talk to an Army recruiter about going into the armed service. That is what Misty had always wanted to do since graduating high school. She went to talk with a recruiter about trying to reenlist into the Army. The recruiter told Misty to come back later on in the week to retake the ASVAB test so she could see what her MOS would be. Misty told the director of whom she worked for about a decision she had made about going into the Army. She felt that it would be a great opportunity for her and her sons. They would have the medical benefits for health coverage, and she could have a career that pays for school to advance in the military.

Misty had called Michael to inform him about the decision she made about trying to get into the Army and would be coming to celebrate Jordan's second birthday. As they continued the conversation on the phone, Misty explained that she would be able to support and take care of her boys by going into the military and that this was a dream of hers to always join the military. She then went on to tell him that she didn't want to depend on the system, because that just wasn't her.

Once Misty got off the phone with Michael it was time for her to go take the ASVAB test. Once she completed it, she got her score right away. Misty had a high score. She chose to take the position as a Human Resource specialist. When it was all over,

Misty felt a relief that she would finally be able to have a secure job to properly take care of her sons. Jordan had a birthday coming up and Misty wasn't going to miss it for the world. Misty was preparing to go and surprise Jordan for his second birthday. She had shirts made for Jordan to wear during his birthday party celebration. Misty was proud of herself as well as her mom. She thanked her mom for encouraging her to continue following the dreams she had abandoned to follow through on after high school.

Chapter Six

Marriage

When Misty made it to Florida, they celebrated Jordan's second birthday. She planned on staying there for a couple months. While Misty was still in Florida visiting, she and Michael started to rekindle old flames. Michael asked his parents what they thought about him proposing to Misty? Surprisingly, his mom and dad were all for the idea of them getting married.

Misty hadn't told her parents she and Michael had come to an understanding of how they should move forward being that they already had two children together. Misty felt uniting her family would be the best thing for them both and it would make basic training and her job much easier, knowing that her family would be joining later.

Misty started feeling pretty good about everything and things were beginning to look up for her. She chose to drive back home and tell the news to her parents face to face, in hopes of getting their approval. Misty called her mom on the phone to ask, "if she and her dad were going to be home over the upcoming weekend?"

"Yes, we will be home," her mother answered. "Why do you ask?"

"Misty explained to her mom that she had something important to talk to them about." Her mom replied, "As long as you're not coming to tell us that you're pregnant again!" "you're good!"

"No, Ma," Misty said.

When Misty got off the phone with her mom, she had a butterfly moment, as if her belly was in a knot. She couldn't believe it herself! After all, Michael put her through! Out of nowhere he asked for her hand in marriage! The weekend was upon them, as they packed the car and got on the road. Misty was nervous. She knew that her parents felt some type of way about how Michael and his family treated her. On the way to share with her parents; what she hoped to be good news Misty knew it could go bad. When Misty, the boys, and Michael had arrived at her parents' house, she was greeted with a hug as she entered the door. Michael followed behind her along with Jordan and Darius.

Misty sat at the kitchen table with Michael and asked her parents "what they thought about her and Michael getting married before she would have to leave for basic training?" Sharon was shocked and didn't like the idea at all, but Misty's father seemed to be ok with it. Sharon felt like the only reason Michael was asking for Misty's hand in marriage was because she was enlisted into the Military, and it would give him financial security. This would take him off the hook of being responsible to properly provide for his sons. Still, Misty tried to convince her mom that this was what she had been wanting to do, and that she had always felt that Michael would be her husband someday.

At this point, there was nothing left for Sharon to say. "Well, Misty," Sharon began, "if this is what you really want to do then hey, you're a grown young lady and you two already have two sons to raise. No matter what me or your father has to say about your decision, you're still going to do what you want to do anyways with or without our permission."

Although Sharon didn't like the idea of them getting married so soon with Misty starting a career in the Armed Services, there was really nothing she was able to do but wish the best for the both of them. Sharon felt that they should have taken time to nourish their relationship, especially since they chose to start fresh after already not doing so well together in the past. Misty informed her parents that she had decided to just stay in Florida with Michael and the boys for the rest of her time as a civilian. She only had 2 more months left to get all her affairs in order before her departure and then she'd be off to basic training.

Misty decided that she and Michael should go to the justice of peace to make everything official. She also mentioned to her parents that although she would love for them to attend, she understood that it was short notice and they had other obligations that would cause them to miss out on a special moment in her life. She knew if they could be there, they would.

No matter how bad Sharon wanted to be there to support her all grown up baby girl, she understood the demand of her job wouldn't allow her to take off with such a short notice. Misty could see that her mom was feeling bad about having to miss attending her wedding. Misty reassured her mom that everything would be ok. She tried to comfort her mother's worry that she was leaving her alone in good hands by letting her know that Michael's parents would be there with her, so she wouldn't be totally alone on her special day.

Sharon started to feel a little better about the situation and she knew that Misty was going to be just fine because she already loved feeling like she was part of Michael's family this time around. Well, the following week they were married. They also made plans to attend Michael's cousin's wedding in the city that weekend. When they made it to the city, they checked into the hotel they would be staying in along with his parents. This is where things started to look a little less beautiful for the newlyweds.

After the first night of the hotel stay, Misty went to withdraw money from the ATM machine. When she looked down at her receipt, the balance that she saw was incorrect. She noticed that she had a large amount of money missing from her personal bank account. That was money she had already saved up from her previous jobs before getting married. Once she made it back to the hotel she asked, "Michael if he withdrew a large amount of money from her account without her knowledge?" He told her yes, "and that he owed his parents the money from almost a year ago." Misty was furious!! "She told Michael that the money she had was just enough for them to live off of until she left for the Armed Services and that her money didn't have anything to do with his own previous debt, especially to his parents before they were married."

"Michael informed Misty now that they were married, her money was his money as well." Misty asked, who told you that? "He told her his mom told him that! She told him that once they were married, her money was his money and his money was her money, and that any money that would be made by either party belonged to the them both." Misty was not buying that part at all. She was having a really hard time understanding how he could just think it was ok to go into her purse; take her bank card and pull out a large amount of cash to pay his parents a debt he owed before they even thought about marriage, and not discuss that bit of information with her first. Misty was really PISSED at this moment! They stayed till the wedding was over. Then they drove back to Michaels parents where they were residing as a married couple.

Although they were currently living with his parents, neither one of them were working. Still, Misty was contributing to the household until it was time for her to leave. His parents had already planned and offered to let them stay at their home while she got ready for basic training, and that Michael, Jordan, and Darius would stay with them until Misty completed the required training. At the time they both thought it would be a great idea, and Misty figured they could save money and buy furniture etc., that they may need once they were at her new duty station after training.

The weeks went by quickly and soon Misty had to say goodbye to her sons. She was sad about having to leave them as young as they were. Jordan was 2 years old and Darius 1. Misty was heartbroken, but at the end of the day she felt in her heart that she was making the best decision for her family. A week before Misty was to leave for basic training, she found out that her husband Michael had another child by another woman while she was pregnant with Darius. She was so hurt, and she really didn't know how to handle the information while she was getting ready to leave. She was hoping for a better future for her family. It just made it so much worse that Michael didn't tell her about this other child before they were married.

She found out by scrolling through his phone one day and came across some pictures. When she asked him about it, he didn't deny anything that Misty had asked him concerning an outside child he had with the other woman. In Misty's opinion, that was something he should have shared with her before marriage. Although it hurt Misty, she didn't let it get her down. It just made her much stronger for the mission in the armed service to do all she could to make sure that her sons were taken care of and would have a better future. After what Michael pulled Misty felt that she couldn't trust him with taking care of financial matters.

Misty called her mom before she left. Sharon could tell something was not right with Misty, while they are having a conversation on the phone. The only thing Misty told her mom was that she was going to be ok. Sharon advised Misty to make sure that she kept God first in whatever situation she finds herself in, even if she's not able to share with her what was going on in her marriage. She also let Misty know that as her mom she will always be that ear to hear whenever she decides to talk about it. She comforted Misty by telling her, "That God already knew what was going on and that he would bring her through any and all things as long as she kept her faith in him."

Misty had already made some important decisions in her preparation to leave. While she was still talking to her mother, she informed her that one of the decisions that she had made was to keep her assigned over all her finances. Misty had a car note and other bills that needed to be paid prior to getting married. She didn't trust Michael with such a responsibility as to handle their finances after the stunt he pulled at the hotel. She knows that she can trust and count on her mother to get things done. Her mother has always had her best interest at heart always given but has never taken from her. When Michael found out about Misty putting her mom in charge of her financial affairs, he was not happy at all to say the least. He was highly upset!

Although her mother was going to take care of her financial affairs, she set up an allotment for Michael and the boys to receive money automatically for items infants and toddlers would need at such a young age. That turns out not to be good enough for Michael. He was upset because he wanted to be in control of all the bank accounts, especially the main account that Misty had already set up for her payments even before the marriage.

When the big day finally came for Misty to complete her paperwork. Michael, Jordan, Darius, and Michael's parents went with Misty to the recruiter station. While they were in the recruiter office with her, Michael overheard the recruiter discussing with Misty about a fifteen thousand dollar signing bonus. When she was signing her paperwork, his eavesdropping was confirmed, he saw it written out in plain English that she was getting a fifteen thousand dollar signing bonus.

After all the final paperwork was complete the next step for Misty was basic training. She was heading to Fort Jackson, South Carolina for a total of three to four months. As they left the recruiter station, Michael asked Misty, "why did her mom have to be over the main account?" Misty explained to Michael, "that her mom's name was already on that account with her before they got married and has always been on the bank account with her." She told him that she was not going to change anything dealing with the way the accounts had been set up, because she couldn't trust him to do the right thing with the money. Misty went on to further let Michael know that it was also the account she would be using for her direct deposits from the Armed Forces.

In May of 2015, Misty left for basic training at Fort Jackson, South Carolina. Jordan and Darius stayed behind with their dad. Misty's mom and dad weren't there to see her off. Although Sharon didn't feel too well about the fact that the boys had to live with their dad while their mom went to join the armed forces in hopes of a better life for her family. Sharon knew that having to deal with small children at such a young age was very demanding and she wondered if Michael was up for the challenge. The boys were used to spending more time with their mom so, with their mom being absent she wondered how things were going to play out. She hoped that Michael would still let the boys come visit them while their mom was away or that he would at least let them have some type of communication with them.

Well, after about a week of Misty being in basic training, Michael reached out to Sharon in a text asking her when she had a chance if she could give him a call. Sharon replied with a text letting him know that she would call him on her lunch break. Sharon didn't know what to think and her mind started racing with thoughts. She wondered if something was wrong with one of the boys because he had never reached out to her before. It was around eight that morning when she received the text. When Sharon took her lunch break around eleven, she went straight out to her car to call Michael.

When she called him, the phone rang twice, he picked up. "Hello Michael," Sharon said, "Is everything ok with the boys?" she asked. He replied yes, the boys were fine! In an aggressive tone." Sharon could hear Jordan in the background crying, and she asked, "Michael why was he crying?" Michael told her that, "he was eating something off the floor, and he took it from him."

"Well," he went on, "I'm just going to come out and ask you!" "Why did Misty put you over the bank account?"

Sharon wasted no time telling Michael that, "Misty has bills of her own and she wanted to make sure that there would be no complications with any of them getting paid, and that Misty knew she could count on her to get things done." "She told him that Misty also knew that she would be able to help her manage the funds for emergency situations."

Sharon went on to say to him, "Now, I don't know what's going on for you to be calling me addressing me about the money situation, but from my understanding she has set you up with an allotment that will have money going straight into your account for you and the boys." "If you need anything more for the boys just let me know and I or Rolanda will make sure that you get it!" We are here for you." Sharon was looking at the time on her phone and saw that her lunch break was over.

Then Sharon asked Michael, "if it would be ok for her to call back once she got off from work to speak with the boys, since her lunch break was over?" "He said that she would be able to." Sharon could tell by the way the phone conversation ended, that Michael was not satisfied with the answers he had just received from her. At that moment she could feel that this was going to cause a problem with whether Michael was going to allow her to have any type of relationship with Jordan and Darius. Sharon prayed that she was wrong, and that Michael wouldn't really take it that far.

Michael was concerned about money that Sharon nor Misty hadn't even received yet. Misty wouldn't get paid for at least another two weeks. That is when Michael would see money in his account for the boys and himself. Michael didn't care about the allotment payments; he was really upset that he wasn't going to be in control of all the money. He was so upset that the second week Misty was in basic training, he went as far as to call her

Drill Sergeant and lie telling them that Misty had left him and the kids without any money or anything in the apartment to eat. He even lied and said that they were getting evicted from their apartment that they allegedly were supposed to be living in. The Drill Sergeant pulled Misty out of formation to ask her about the allegations. "Misty told the Drill Sergeant that her husband and the boys didn't live in an apartment, and that they lived in the home with his parents. She also informed her Drill Sergeant that Michael was told if they needed anything before, she got paid to just call her mom. Misty told the Drill Sergeant that she made sure that her family would be taken care of in the place of her absence." Misty wasn't allowed to get phone privileges until later on in the program, but in this case, she was given permission to call home and get the situation under control.

The first person she called was her mom to find out if Michael had called her with any of that nonsense. "Sharon told her that he hadn't, but that she was not surprised at what he did, because of the phone call she and Michael had a week prior." Sharon suggested that Misty call Michael to find out what's going on, and that if he needs money before she gets paid; tell him to call her. Misty didn't know what to think about her new husband. She knew that money could make people show their true hidden self. Misty and Sharon just couldn't understand how a person could be causing so much confusion about money that hadn't even been paid out yet. Who was to say if she would even be receiving a check directly after basic training? Anything could happen before then. The way he interfered with her job could have really cost her chances of achievement to spiral down. Making all her goals and dreams to become a soldier in hopes of a better future for her sons unaccomplished.

By the third week of Misty being in basic training, she was able to start having phone privileges. Sharon had been calling Michael to check on Jordan and Darius but hadn't really been able to talk with them much. Michael either wouldn't answer the phone or would say they were asleep. When Misty called her mom, they would discuss the last time they had any contact with the boys. Michael had started taking his feelings to an entirely different level by keeping the boys away from them. Michael didn't have a job, so there wasn't any excuse for him to not answer the phone when Misty would call!

It wasn't okay for Michael to start keeping Misty from having any contact with their kids, all because he was still in his feelings about the money situation. As Misty continued basic training, she tried to stay positive, but it was hard for her knowing that she had married someone she really thought she knew, but obviously didn't!

Sometimes Michael would call Sharon out of the blue to complain about money but wouldn't let her speak to the boys. Sharon told Michael, "That Misty was sending him as much money as she could

81

with the little that she makes right now without them going broke." "They had to have money for the duty station they were being assigned to." Misty had been assigned to Germany for a two-year tour. Sharon had asked Michael "if he was going to get a job to help Misty out?" He stated, "he was looking." Then he went into his feelings and said, "Misty has someone to help her pay her bills!" ``I have bills that need to be paid with no help!" Sharon asked Michael' "what bills he had, and how much were they?" She was going to see what she could do to help him, but Michael never gave her a number.

Then he mentioned that he wasn't feeling well and needed to go see a doctor. So, Sharon reminded him that he had a military ID card to go on post for medical treatment with no extra cost. Michael claimed that Misty hadn't completed the necessary paperwork for him to go get his ID card. "Well, how much will it be for you to go to urgent care?" Sharon asked, but Michael still wouldn't give a number. He just seemed to be very agitated.

Sharon felt that he was stressed about something and very desperate, but he wasn't saying anything about it. At this point Sharon was very fearful for the kids.

Michael had texted Misty a message that would bring anyone to tears. The text message read: "I feel like I'm just your stuff keeper and a babysitter." Misty didn't understand how he could text that to her when she had clearly put her life on the line for their family. She was doing everything she could to make their life better, though he wouldn't even get a job and wasn't in a rush to find one. *"Where is the teamwork?"* Misty thought.

Misty was under the impression that Michael was going to get a job to help out with the needs of their family while she was away as well. All this pettiness and uncertainty of whether Michael would allow her to see or talk to the boys was driving her crazy. At this point Misty hadn't been able to FaceTime the boys in a month. Her mom had been trying to make plans to visit, but Michael wasn't allowing it and she rarely got to talk to them on the phone either. One evening, Sharon was home from work when she received a call from Michael's mom, (Brenda). To Sharon it was quite a surprise that she called her. When Sharon answered the phone, Brenda started in on her immediately.

"Now Sharon, you know that the money Misty is sending for the kids is not enough money!" "My husband and I spend double that a month on the boys." "Do you really think that's enough money?"

Sharon wasn't having it. In reply to Brenda's rudeness, "Misty is one person, and you know she doesn't make enough money to take care of everything; when she's just starting without any rank!" "She's doing the best she can to support her family." Sharon stated, "We don't like living paycheck to paycheck." "she's trying to make sure they have money for the move." "Why won't Michael just go get a job and help her?"

Brenda fired back! "He doesn't need to get a job." "They will be leaving when Misty comes home!"

"ARE YOU SERIOUS?" Sharon asked. That was the keyword to end that conversation.

Sharon was really bothered by the nerve of another mother condoning a grown man not working to help support his family. "Like, where do they do that?" "Oh yeah that's the new millennial," Thought Sharon. Sharon just didn't know how to wrap her head around that one. They were concerned about the wrong thing, where were the kids in all this? It had been a month and a half Sharon still hadn't seen Jordan and Darius. Even Misty was having very little communication with them.

Michael was still calling starring up drama for Misty. This time he reached out to her commander complaining about money! He even went as far as to lie about her not calling her children when he clearly had been ignoring her phone calls every Sunday that she was allowed to call home. Michael was calling the Commander so often that Misty had to be counseled. He must not have been thinking that if she got kicked out, there would be no money. Sharon wondered what Misty had gotten her and the boys into. She went from seeing or talking to the kids daily to barely being able to talk to them even seldomly. Sharon was a very family-oriented person, she loved her grandkids as if they were her own. She had become very depressed with not knowing when she would ever hear from her grandsons again.

Chapter Seven

A Grandmother's Love

Sharon not being able to see or hear from Jordan and Darius for three months off and on caused her to bombard both Michael and Brenda's phones nonstop; but that didn't make them answer the phones. Yet she was determined to see her grandsons; they could not ignore her forever.

Eventually Michael finally answered the phone and agreed to let Sharon choose a day to come pick the boys up and keep them for a week. What Michael didn't know was that Sharon was going to see if he would like to join the boys and stay a week as well. Sharon had reserved a room at the recently built Value Inn downtown for him to have his own space for the entire stay while the boys were visiting. The visit was to take place in July after Sharon came back from her family reunion. She was so excited she could hardly wait, oh how she longed to see them. It warmed her heart, although Michael had been putting limitations on any communication concerning the boys. That didn't matter to Sharon. Any little time she could spend with the boys she was willing to take. Before then even though Michael wasn't answering any phone calls or text messages; Their mom, Sharon and Rolanda would send care boxes to the boys. The boxes contained various items: diapers, wipes, and clothes. Sharon and Rolanda would inform Misty of the items that were sent to the boys, vice versa, but neither one of them would know whether or not they were received. They would have to ask Misty when they spoke to her if Michael ever mentioned the packages that they would send the boys. Misty didn't have an answer for them at times because she was treated the same way when it came to the boys. Michael wasn't giving anyone any answers.

Beyond all of that, it didn't make Sharon's heart feel good knowing how Michael was handling things in Misty's absence. Sharon still had no hard feelings against Michael at all nor his parents, she just wanted to see her grandsons. She didn't understand the level of how far he was willing to take things and wondered what the real reason was behind his actions. Sharon tried not to think about it too much, she was just excited that he agreed on some type of communication. Regardless of how long it had been. Michael would never know just how much pain he caused Sharon. It was extremely difficult for her not being able to interact in any kind of way with her grandsons. The distance of the drive made it impossible to visit the boys unannounced.

Rolanda lived out of state with her family, and they lived even farther away than Jordan and Darius. As Sharon prepared for the family reunion that was coming up that weekend, she was also preparing for her time with the boys. She was so excited; anyone could see her smiling from a mile away, cheek to cheek with all her teeth showing.

The day finally came to leave for the family reunion. Sharon and her family would be there for two days and be returning on that Sunday. Then Monday of that week, Sharon and her sister-in-law would be driving another eight and a half hours to go pick up Michael, Jordan, and Darius to spend the week with them. She was so unimaginably happy, with joy in her heart.

Once they arrived to pick up the boys, they noticed what they thought was Michael and the boys leaving with his parents in a car passing theirs on the way out. Sharon wasn't sure if it was them or not because they had gotten a new vehicle and she didn't recognize it. They ended up turning around and coming back to their house, because they recognized Sharon while they were passing by.

Once the two parties met up, Sharon was sure that Michael was going to let her get the boys. Then she could let him know that she made preparations for him to come also. Michael's parents parked and let the boys out of the vehicle. Sharon was so happy, but Darius didn't remember her as well as Jordan did despite it only being a few months since they'd seen her. Sharon asked Michael "where the boy's clothes were?" Michael responded that "their clothes were in the house, but he told her that they were not going." He proceeded to tell Sharon that if he hadn't heard anything from Misty about the conversation they had with the money situation, that he was going to take action against her. He said that "he was headed to a very important meeting out of town when he saw her coming and turned around. "

Sharon was so hurt, and heart broken when she couldn't get the boys. She asked Michael "if he was keeping the kids from her because of what he and Misty had going on about the money?" Michael told Sharon, "That he didn't mean any disrespect to her, but that it was between him and his wife!"

Sharon got upset and she told him, "I drove all these hours to pick up my grandsons and spend time with them because I hadn't seen them in months, and now you're trying to tell me I can't get them?"

"Well, I haven't heard from Misty the whole weekend," Michael replied.

Sharon said, "You know that she was in the field this week, and they couldn't have their phones." Sharon asked again!" "Are you all trying to keep my grandsons from me?"

"What do you mean by you all?" Brenda interjected. "I had no idea that you were coming to pick them up or I would have had Jordan ready."

Sharon included her in the issue because of their previous phone call. When she called on behalf of her son talking about Misty not sending enough money, she felt that they were all in cahoots together. She felt that while her daughter was out there working hard for the family, they were condoning their son's actions of not contributing to the marriage or household!

Sharon was there for about a good fifteen to twenty minutes going back and forth with Michael and Brenda instead of spending time with her grandsons. Sharon rode all the way back home in disappointment. She didn't know what kind of people she was having to deal with or who in the world Misty had added into their family. Who does the things that they were doing? Why couldn't Michael understand that Misty and her family weren't trying to do anything but take care of their family the best way they knew how?

Michael had to realize that he didn't know how to manage the account properly, so why be mad at Misty for not risking their financial stability and becoming broke? The arrangement would only be until Misty completed basic training, and in the end, it was going to benefit their family.

During the visit, Michael even lashed out at Sharon, yet she still chose to see that there was something in him that was screaming for help. She didn't take it personally, although it would be hard for most people, but anyone who knew her and the kind of heart she has would know that Sharon didn't have it in her to be spiteful no matter how heartbroken she was feeling and regardless of what was happening. She would just continue to say that they didn't know any better. She believed that this storm would come to pass someday and that she would be able to see her grandsons and talk with them as freely as she wanted to. She believed that once Misty completed basic training and made it back home, everything would be alright again. All of her belief came from the faith she has in God.

Sharon had a talk with Michael earlier on during this journey that if he didn't stop causing problems at Misty's job about money, he was going to mess around and ruin his marriage before it even got started. But he just wouldn't listen! As he continued to call and make problems for Misty in the military. It was going to be a long drive back home for Sharon. She is saddened, but still holding on to her faith in God that things would get better.

Her faith was something She had always kept with her no matter what was happening in her life. It was hard to recover from the bad experience She had with Michael, but with God she can overcome anything.

Soon weeks had gone by, and it was time for Misty to graduate from basic training at Fort Jackson in South Carolina. Although Sharon hadn't really spoken to Michael since the ordeal at his parents' house, she reached out to Michael to see if he knew the day of Misty's graduation and to find out if he and the boys would need a ride. To Sharon's surprise, he responded back in a text saying yes, he would like to go but he will need a ride. Sharon kindly offered to allow him and the boys to ride with her and her husband." he agreed.

Sharon had to make arrangements for Michael and the boys to get from their house to hers, which was about eight in a half hours. Then they all would have to get up early the next morning and drive about eight more hours to make it in time for graduation. For a moment, Sharon was feeling whole again; not only was she getting to spend time with Jordan and Darius, but her daughter Rolanda and other grandkids were going to meet them there. Sharon was going to have all her grandkids in one place for the first time in a long time.

When they arrived at Fort Jackson, it was very exciting for Sharon to see all the family together again. To her it has always been a beautiful thing! There was nothing like family to Sharon. When you look at her, she is all smiles. To see All that she had gone through with Michael those past few months didn't compare to the joy she was feeling in her heart at that moment. Anytime that she got to spend with her family; negativity didn't matter. She was determined to just live in the moment and sit back thanking God and enjoying the greatest accomplishment of her life, which was the family that God blessed her with.

While they were together, everyone checked into their rooms. Then they all went to meet up with

Misty. When they found her, it was like a family reunion. Jordan and Darius were happy to see their mom. Misty was equally happy if not happier to see her sons. They were able to see their mom in her uniform. Misty's boys seeing her in a military uniform makes it very easy for her to explain to her sons what her job was and why she had uniform on. Graduation was the next day. Having her sons get a chance to see her walk out onto the field as one of her accomplishments was the best gift of all.

Misty's day of graduation was bittersweet for Sharon. Her baby girl was all grown up with babies of her own and although she had a hard time in basic, she made it through with the grace of God. Misty introduced some of the people that she graduated with to her family. After graduation, they went out to dinner. While they were out for dinner, Michael brought up the account situation again with Misty in a private conversation. He gave her an ultimatum: either she puts him on the account and takes her mom off, or they're done! That just made

Misty mad, because she wasn't understanding what the fuss was all about. She made sure he got funds put into his bank account every two weeks. He wasn't working so why was he so upset about money he wasn't helping to bring into their household? She didn't know what else to do, and the way he had been acting since she's been gone was unacceptable. She was still upset about him keeping her sons from her family and avoiding her phone calls.

Michael couldn't let Misty enjoy her day. This was supposed to be a time to celebrate her accomplishment of making it through basic training and doing something that many people don't have a chance to. Basic training was no joke. The next morning everyone met up at the recreation center for the whole family to play games. Once they were done, they all packed up to leave. It was hard for Sharon to let go of how she was feeling at that moment, to see her family separated again. The only thing that she was able to hold on to is her faith in

God to know that soon everything would be ok! As they all loaded the kids into the vehicles, Misty was taken back to the barracks and they all said, "See you soon!"

As they drove off; Sharon could feel the tension in the vehicle as they rode back from graduation with Michael and the boys in the car. When Sharon and John dropped Michael and the boys off at his parents' house, she hated to depart from them because she was rehashing the heartache all over again as she reflected back remembering not being able to see them for months. You could tell Michael wasn't present by the look on his face the whole entire ride. Once they made it to his parents' house, he got out of the vehicle without any eye contact, said a brief and dry goodbye. No one could see what was happening but Sharon. She had tears in her eyes, while the boys got out of the car heading into the house as they drove off, her heart was heavy. She was broken having to leave her grandsons again. Sharon was beginning to wonder if it was going to ever end.

The next day, Sharon tried calling Michael's cell phone to make sure that they would have some form of communication after their trip to graduation, but once again he ignored her call. Misty didn't have but a few weeks left at basic before she was to return home and report to her new duty station. By then her location had changed from Germany to South Seoul, Korea. Because of all the phone calls and allegations Michael had continued to make throughout Misty's training during her entire time in basic, she was forced to tell the commander that she and Michael were heading towards a divorce.

It had come down to either her career or her marriage. She had to choose one to let go. Misty chose her marriage because Michael didn't leave her any choice. She worked too hard to make it through basic to turn around and get put out of the military for a bunch of lies surrounding his greed.

Meanwhile, Sharon was in a horrible state of mind wondering how the boys were doing. It got to the point once again where the phone calls continued to be ignored as she would call in hopes of talking to her grandsons. Misty wasn't going to have a lot of time once she made it home from basic training. She only has a week to spend with her sons before going off to Korea. Misty had never been out of the country before. When she got home, she went to pick up her sons to visit with her parents, but Michael wouldn't allow her to pick them up and leave without him. Misty called her mom to let her know that it was going to be a problem trying to spend time with them and her sons. Michael wouldn't allow her to take the boys out of state to visit them. Sharon told Misty it was okay if she was not able to bring them as long as she had a chance to spend time with her sons, is all that matters. Sharon advised Misty to pray and be strong. She wanted her to know that no matter what, God was with her regardless of what the situation looked like and her circumstances at this time as she has reiterated to her in the past.

Sharon was doing her best to try and encourage Misty, but the words of advice she was giving Misty were the words that she needed to embrace for herself. Inside, Sharon was in a lot of heartache, pain, a reck and a mess. She was very depressed on the inside, and no one could tell how much this was eating at her. When a grandmother loves, she loves hard. Sharon had a love for her family, just like the old school grandmothers did back in the day. You didn't cross that line to mistreat their family members, not without some words of wisdom. Seeing their grandkids was a must. Misty was showing better strength than Sharon when it came down to her having to go so far away from her sons and leaving them with that turmoil of a family she had married into. Oh, how Sharon wished it was different for Misty. It was like Sharon's heart had been tied into a knot. It had gotten so bad that Sharon could barely sleep at night or complete house chores without thinking about her daughter and grandsons. It had come close to a year since she last saw her grandsons and she was dying inside.

While Misty was over in Korea, not only were Sharon and the family cut off from the boys, but Misty was cut off as well. Sharon wasn't only worrying about her grandsons anymore; she was thinking about her daughter's state of mind and well-being because she was so far away in another country and couldn't do anything. Misty had signed up for something way more demanding. It was honorable of her to help serve and protect the country.

Michael wouldn't even let her FaceTime her sons, all while he was still getting an allotment. Misty started having her sister call Michael for a welfare check of her sons. Once she started doing that, Michael would call her that same day as if he hadn't done anything wrong. A grandmother's love for their grandchildren can come in all kinds of ways; it doesn't just have to be a paternal grandchild. It could be a foster child or adopted child. In this instance, Sharon's pain was related to her pain for her daughter Misty, as well as for her grandsons. Sharon couldn't imagine the depth of suffering that had been imposed on her daughter. She couldn't imagine not being able to speak or hear from Misty so far away while in another country; not knowing if she was okay or not?

Sharon advises Misty to continue trying to reach out to Michael. She replied to her mom that, "he had a new phone number and that she tried calling his parents' house phone; no one would pick up!" Sharon could tell that Misty was exhausted from this whole ordeal. Sharon wondered to herself if there was anyone besides herself that thought the whole thing was absurd. She couldn't help but wonder how and why this had gone so far. Sharon's faith was growing weak. She was so stressed from not being able to see or hear from her grandsons that it took a toll on her health. Sharon had become depressed and sick from all the stress she found herself under.

She had experienced stress once before, but never to the point that she had gotten sick or depressed for a long period of time. All the nonsense was just driving her insane. At the same time, Michael got to the point that he was calling to Korea spreading lies while still getting money put into the account that she had set up for him almost a year and eight months ago.

With all the confusion going on, Sharon hadn't realized how fast time had flown bye. She was hurting inside, her heart's longing to see her grandsons. It was starting to feel like she would never see them again. By this time, not only had they not been answering phone calls from the house phone, but they changed their cell phone numbers. Something had to be done. Rolanda advised Misty that it was time to get the police involved to do a welfare check on the boys again. When the police were called to do a welfare check, they found out that Michael and his parents no longer reside at that address anymore.

Sharon didn't have any grandparent rights to the boys by law. She found out by calling around to different attorney offices for some legal advice for grandparents' visitation or rights. They all told her the same thing: that grandparents don't have rights to their grandchildren legally. Sharon was not giving up, no matter what it took to try and find her grandsons. She was now also focused on getting some type of grandparent rights. But there was really nothing that could be done while the boys were in another state living with their dad and their mom was out of the country.

Misty finally decided to follow through with the divorce from Michael as he left her with no other choice. He was doing the most by still causing problems while she was in Korea. Misty and Sharon had to come to terms that at that point it all boiled down to Michael being money hungry, as well as him attempting to control Misty by totally cutting her off from her sons. Misty asked her mom, "if she could find a lawyer?" Sharon replied, "yes, if this is what you think is best." As she started the mission of trying to find a good divorce and family Attorney, they mentioned that if Misty came back to the states to visit or stay, she wouldn't be allowed to get her sons back from Michael nor leave the state with her sons. It seemed that Michael had the ball in his court. Sharon and Misty were lost for words. But that didn't stop their determination to fight for custody of the boys.

Sharon started gathering all the evidence she could find against Michael in hopes of hiring a good Attorney to take on the case. After a few phone calls in one day, Sharon had found an Attorney in the state where Michael lived. They knew he still lived in the state, just a different address. Rolanda joined in on the search for locating the boys. She called and spoke to a clerk at the civil courts office and was able to get Information on how to proceed in locating a person's new location of residency. The clerk from civil court who advised Rolanda to send a proof of residency letter on behalf of Misty. Michael had thirty days to respond.

While Rolanda continued trying to help Misty locate the whereabouts of her sons, Sharon was doing her part as far as the legal side of things. She was trying to retain an Attorney that would agree to take on the case. In reference to doing so they needed to speak with Misty to get more information about the situation to further proceed with whether or not they would take her case being that she's in another country. To do so, Misty had to set up telephone conferences during a convenient time for the Attorney. Going through this process felt like a nightmare to Sharon, and she wondered when she was going to wake up. But it wasn't a nightmare; this was happening for real.

Sharon's heart was getting a lot heavier as the days and weeks rolled by without knowing where or how her grandsons were doing or if they were ok! One-night Sharon went to bed with a very heavy heart. She couldn't help but to look at the situation from the perspective that Michael might get away with taking the boys away from them for good, and that she and Misty may never see them again. She couldn't bear the thought of it! Tears rolled daily from her eyes when she thought about her precious grandbabies.

For Sharon's own good, she had to get to the point of not thinking about the boys at all. Doing this was going to be the only way for her to take care of her health. She had to block out Jordan and Darius, if she didn't want to continue bringing harm to her body with all the stress that had turned into depression. A few nights later she was preparing for bed. The first thing she did was, she got down on her knees to pray, rolled the covers back, got into the bed and went to sleep. As Sharon slept God showed her in a dream that all was well, he showed her in court as if it was already over and that she would see her grandsons again. Her dream showed her that she was also going to win in the courtroom and that she and Misty were going to get to spend all the time they desired with the boys.

When Sharon awoke the next morning, she said out loud, "amen, praise the Lord, thank you Jesus." This was God's way of giving Sharon confirmation that everything was going to work out and he hadn't forgotten about her. Later, that day, Sharon paid the requested retainer fee of two thousand dollars to the Attorney. She also sent any and all documentations that could be used for the divorce and child custody case. Sharon informed Misty of how much the Attorney needed up front to get the ball rolling and it had been paid. She informed Misty that the Attorney would be contacting her with scheduled conferences as they had discussed during their inquiry process.

Then, through their own initial contact with Misty, the Attorney told her that they will keep her updated with every step in the case. Misty asked, "if there was any way that they could send something to the judge that would force Michael to form some type of communication with her so she could FaceTime her sons, or at least talk to them on the phone?" The Attorney told Misty, "That there wasn't anything they could do until court papers were filed and that her being in another country wasn't helping her case because the boys were with their biological dad."

Misty asked all kinds of questions. She wanted to know how she could possibly be punished by the court for her job overseas. She didn't understand how that could very well cause her to lose her sons. Sharon still found herself torn up about the situation with her daughter and grandsons. She had just gotten to a point where she wished it was all over. She saw how hard Misty was fighting to try and see her sons and she understood how Misty could be feeling or any mother for that matter having to go through something like this. It's almost like asking her to choose between her sons and her job. A job that helps put clothes on their back and medical insurance if they get sick. Sharon loved all her grandchildren as if they were her own children. They were her world and although she hadn't borne them, they were her daughters' children, and she loves them both just the same but love for your grandchildren it's a little different. Not to say that she didn't love her daughters; she just recognized that it was a different type of love. She saw how much pain this was causing her family and she hated that they had to sit back and TRY to rely on the system to see if it was going to work for their good. She knew that it was more than their faith and patience that was being tested. They had to learn to trust God.

After about three months with the law firm Sharon had chosen to take them off the case; she felt they had turned out to be more of a headache than helping to solve the problem. There was a via mediation appointment set up for Michael and Misty. The Lawyer was supposed to sit in mediation on Misty's behalf while she was still in Korea. Misty had to join in by phone instead of physically being there. They basically sat in that room during the meeting and didn't speak up for Misty at all. When the mediation was over, Misty was told by her Attorney that Michael had a better chance at keeping their sons than the judge awarding her custody. Sharon seemed to be just as upset about this crazy talk than Misty. The law firm that Sharon had chosen was a mess and no help at all.

Chapter Eight

Best Lawyer
Money Could Buy

Even though things weren't looking good for Sharon and Misty, this was no time at all for a pity party. Sharon couldn't allow this to make her doubt what God had already shown her. She just needed to stay the course and do what needed to be done on her end and trust the process. Misty didn't understand why her mom was so calm about the way the Attorney handled her mediation process. Misty felt like that was the only opportunity she had to finally see her sons. She didn't know that her mom had started looking for another law firm to take the case. Sharon soon found a law firm while strolling online that met all the qualifications for a family court case. She looked and read all the reviews. This law firm was given five stars from all their clients. When Sharon saw how much it was going to cost for a retainer fee she nearly panicked until she remembered, God has his hands on this case. Yes, it was a little more expensive than the first law firm, but as the old saying goes, *"you get what you pay for."*

In the meantime, Misty continued the process of trying to get back to the states to fight for her sons. Misty still couldn't believe that Michael actually took it this far over money. She was even more upset with herself that she didn't see it early on before the marriage. As far as she could remember there were no warning signs there! When Sharon came to Misty with the idea of getting another Attorney, she wasn't on board. She told her mom that, "they had just paid out a total of eight-thousand five hundred dollars to the law firm that was currently still representing them." Sharon told Misty, "That she knew that, but with the way things were looking with their current Attorney she wasn't doing anything to help them." "It looked as if they were helping Michael's case. Sharon further explained, "that she didn't like the way they were handling the case and how they had Misty all stressed out."

Sharon also told Misty, "That she wasn't happy about wasting money that had already been spent on the wrong firm, but she was confident that God would guide them to the right law firm just for their case." She told Misty, "That she had already seen the new law firm they needed to retain for the case." Sharon advised Misty, "that they would have to do whatever they had to do, to get a different law firm, because they couldn't keep wasting money on a law firm that was practically helping Michael to win."

"We can do better, and this time the money we use to retain the next Attorney will be well worth it because right now we have wasted time and money with this Attorney." "Sharon said," Her grandsons were worth every dime she had to spend."

About a week after this conversation, Misty told her mom, "that her orders had been approved to return to the states so that she can take care of her personal business." Sharon was really glad to hear that! She knew it would make things a lot easier having her back in the states and she felt that maybe now they both would have the opportunity to go and see Jordan and Darius. Misty and her mom had no idea what was about to happen next. *You couldn't make this up if you wanted to* ......

A few days after Misty returned to the states, she and her mom called to schedule a free consultation with the prospective new law firm. The appointment had been scheduled for the upcoming Friday for nine in the morning. They were prepared to make whatever necessary changes that needed to be made in their case. When it was time to meet with the lawyer, Sharon and Misty talked about seeing what they needed to do to see the boys without causing any confusion while they were in town.

The week seemed to be going by slowly! Misty and Sharon could hardly wait until Friday. When Friday did finally come around Misty and Sharon got on the road and were heading down the highway laughing and having small talk about how the boys' personalities may or may not have changed very much in the last two years. Yes! By that time Sharon hadn't seen or spoken to her grandsons in two years. She felt that this moment was going to be beautiful. As they were getting closer to their destination, they talked about taking the boys to a fun place to eat lunch if possible. Soon they arrived at the new law firm. It was very clean and elegant looking inside, on the outside of the building it looked new. Everyone was nice and professional. After sitting for about 5 minutes, it was time to meet with the Attorney. Once in the back, Misty did all the talking, and when she was done talking the Attorney stated that she would be interested in taking on the case. She also shared with them her retainer fee cost and how she handles her clients' cases. She was upfront with Sharon and Misty by explaining that their contract doesn't guarantee they'll win the case, but that she always gives it everything she's got. She told them, "that no lawyer can guarantee they're going to win a case, but she could guarantee that she was going to do everything she could to win."

The new Attorney told Misty the process of how to get started if she decided to go forth with her firm. Misty and Sharon left the attorney's office and were very pleased with what they discussed. Misty decided they were going to see if they could spend the day with the boys and stay overnight in a hotel so visiting them wouldn't seem rushed. Before reaching the residence that Michael and his parents had moved to, Misty got on the phone to try and call Michael but there was no answer. Misty called a second time, this time leaving a message to let him know that she was on her way to see Jordan and

Darius in hopes of spending time with them. When Misty didn't reach Michael on his cell phone, she tried calling one of his parents' cell phones but also got no answer. By this time, she was in the neighborhood. Misty was hoping that someone would call her back or answer their phone, but neither happened!

When they drove up to the house, Misty pulled into the driveway. The house was much bigger than the house they moved out of. As Misty was getting out of the car to approach the front door, Sharon took out her cell phone to record. Misty asked, "What are you doing?" Sharon responded, "that she was going to record, because they really didn't know Michael and his parents." She continued saying we need to protect ourselves with all the lies and manipulation they have done." Sharon didn't trust them and just wanted to make sure she and Misty were covered. Misty still insisted that her mom didn't need to do any recording, so she put the phone down, but once

Misty got out of the car, Sharon held the phone up to record. Misty rang the doorbell, no one answered. She knocked on the door, no one answered. Then she rang it again, still no one answered. Then she knocked on the door, again no one answered. After the third try, Misty turned around and headed back towards the car to get in and stated, "I guess no one is in there, they didn't answer the door!"

As Misty backed out the driveway, Sharon was looking at the recording footage. Sharon had caught something going on in the background of the window as Misty was walking away from the porch. Sharon had captured the curtains moving with someone peeping out of the window.

Sharon immediately shouted out, "Misty, there's someone in the house!"

"Ma, I knocked, and no one came to the door," Misty insisted. Sharon showed Misty what she had recorded with her phone. She was glad her mom was recording after she showed her the video.

After that Misty decided to sit in the driveway in hopes of contacting Michael, hoping that if they were in there the pressure of them sitting outside would cause him to pick up the phone this time. But when she called again there was no answer, and she didn't receive a return call either. So, while Misty was still trying to reach Michael to see the boys, guess who showed up? Not Michael, not the grandpa, but the police! That's right, the person that was peeping out of the window was Brenda. She had called the police on Misty.

Sharon told Misty that someone had called the police on her. She didn't think that her mom knew what she was talking about, but then the cops got out of their vehicle, and they walked towards the front door and knocked. Brenda answered the door, opened it, and talked to them. Soon after they had finished talking to Brenda they came out to the curve on the side of the road where Sharon and Misty were parked in front of the residence. Sharon decided to record. The officer came over and asked

Misty who she was. They stated that the lady of the house said they were trespassing and had a restraining order that said Misty could not come to their home.

Misty tried to explain to the officer that she had just come back from Korea and was trying to see her sons that lived there. The officer told her that Brenda informed them that she had custody of her sons and even showed them the court papers. He went on to warn her that she had to leave and if she came back, they would have to arrest her for trespassing. Sharon's heart dropped and she was speechless. It did something to her to hear the policeman say to her child that she couldn't see her own sons. Misty burst out into tears. Sharon told her, "that they will do whatever they had to for her to get her sons back."

As Misty started driving, Sharon asked, "where were they going?" Misty replied, "Home." Sharon told Misty, "to drive over to the Attorney's office that was still handling the case and fire them."

"Then go over to the other law firm and hire the new Attorney." Misty was upset, discouraged, and felt defeated. She didn't want to conduct any more business that day, but this was no time to lay down and give up. It was time to fight even harder. Like, "Satan, get out of my way" type of fighting. Sharon finally convinced Misty that this was the best thing to do. So, after firing that other firm, Sharon and Misty took all the documents relating to the case to the new Attorney and she reassured Misty that she was in good hands.

Sharon was so numb, she didn't have time to grieve for herself even a little, because her daughter needed her now more than ever. When they are young growing up, kids need their mothers. Well, when they are all grown up and become adults, they still need their mothers. The hard part was knowing when to jump in to help and when not to help. This was a moment to jump in and help. Misty was about to lose it. What else was there for a mother to do? A mother sharing in a mother's pain. Next, Sharon did the only thing she knew could comfort her daughter at that time. She prayed for Misty as she watched the tears roll down her cheeks. In that same moment Sharon shed tears as well, but Sharon's tears weren't of sadness. She was feeling the joy of what God had in store that they could not see yet.

After Sharon finished praying, the drive was quiet. There was no talking, no music playing, just a lot of silence the whole ride back. By Monday of the next week, Misty started getting documents from her new Attorney that needed to be signed and filed through the court for an emergency hearing so that she could see her sons. All the sadness that was going on had become smiles of hope. Sharon was feeling good about this Attorney and was confident that she was going to make a big difference, because this time she didn't choose the Attorney; God did!

Soon after that they had their first court hearing, but it didn't seem to go that well because the boys still had to live with Michael. It seemed that the judge was siding with Michael and overlooking the mess he had caused to Misty's family and her career. The judge ordered that Misty could get her sons for visitation on the first, third, and fifth Sunday out of the month. Sharon was just excited to get that, although she knew Misty wanted her sons back right then and there. Sharon was choosing to see how far they had come, from not seeing them for two years to legally being granted the right to see them every other weekend.

This whole ordeal taught Sharon how to be more patient for great things to happen. A couple of months after that court hearing, visitation changed from weekends to every other week. Jordan and Darius still hadn't been assigned custody to their mom yet. It still looked like Michael had everything going in his favor. About six months into the case was the big court date. The day of court both Misty and Sharon were trying to do the best that they could to not show their emotions as they prepared for that day. While in the courtroom, no one from either side spoke to one another. Sharon didn't feel any kind of way towards them, the opportunity just didn't present itself to where she could have spoken.

Although Sharon knew the way they kept her grandsons away from her for no apparent reason other than for the greed of money was wrong, she always just said to herself, "They just don't know any better." She believed that no matter how old a person was, they could still not know any better, and even when they did it was still a choice to do the right thing or not. By the end of court, after everyone had taken the stand, it was time for Judge Ruth to decide.

Judge Ruth said what she needed to say for the plaintiff and the defendant. At the end of the day, it was up to her to decide what she felt was best for Jordan and Darius.

With all the tears, all the back and forth, all the heartache, all the sad days, all the money paid out, in the end there was favor! There was finally relief for Sharon's family. God showed them what being patient, trusting, and having faith in Him to bring about the change that needed to be made got them. That Attorney was the best money they could've ever spent on the case. Misty had won custody of her sons. Walking out of the courtroom, Sharon saw the other grandmother in tears being consoled by their Attorney. She wanted to let them know that it was going to be okay and that they could still participate in the boys' lives. Although Michael and his parents wanted the boys all or nothing, Sharon and Misty didn't feel that way. As Sharon continued to walk on by, she wouldn't wish what they had done to her as a grandparent and Misty as the boy's mom on anyone else including her worst enemy.

Sharon saw that it wasn't the time nor the place to discuss her thoughts with the other grandparents, nor the dad because she didn't think that they would hear her out or was ready to receive what she had to say. Months after Judge Ruth made her ruling in favor of Misty; Sharon couldn't get over the fact that Michaels parents hadn't reached out to see or try to talk to their grandsons that they had kept away from them for two years. One Sunday afternoon Sharon decided to reach out to encourage them to try and put their feelings aside and come together on spending time with their grandsons. She knew that the boys needed all of them and not one side or the other. When she spoke to them, Brenda was shocked, but expressed how grateful she was that Sharon had reached out and the fact that they were willing to allow them into the boys' lives after all that had been said and done.

OTHER BOOKS BY THIS AUTHOR

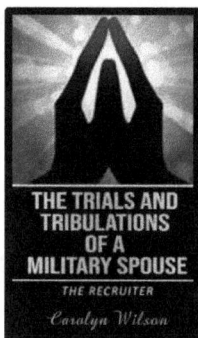

The Trials and Tribulations of a Military Spouse
(The Recruiter)

www.dream-faith.com

SOCIAL MEDIA

(Follow Me)

 @dreamfaith

 Carolyn Wilson/dream faith publishing

 Carolyn

@dreamfaithpublishing

www.ingramcontent.com/pod-product-compliance
Lightning Source LLC
Chambersburg PA
CBHW060908280326
41934CB00007B/1237